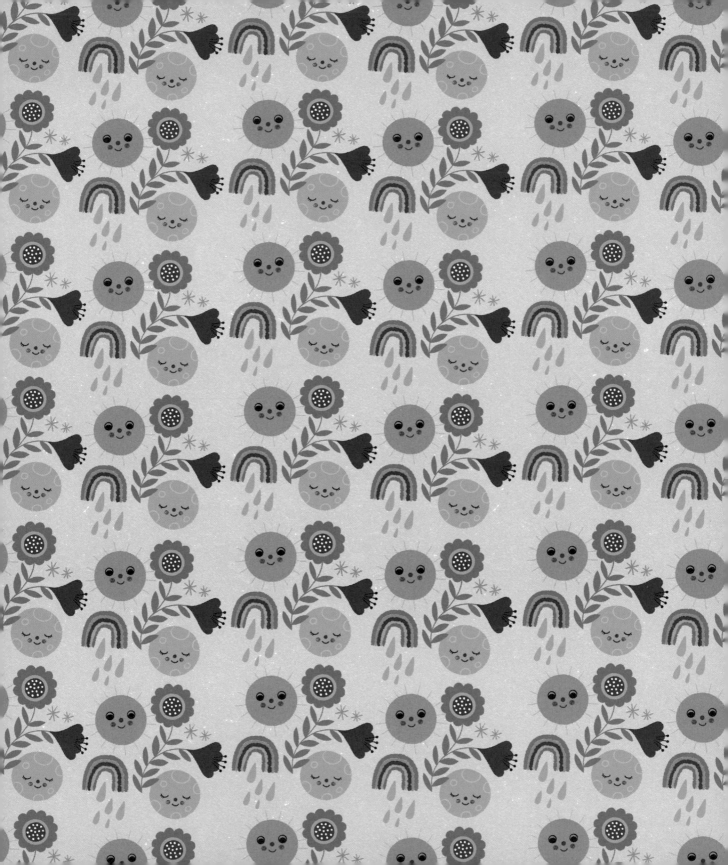

Mindful
Moves

MINDFUL MOVES

Kid-Friendly Yoga and Peaceful Activities for a Happy, Healthy You

Nicole Cardoza

Storey Publishing

The mission of Storey Publishing is to serve our customers by publishing practical information that encourages personal independence in harmony with the environment.

Edited by Deanna F. Cook and Hannah Fries
Art direction and book design by Ash Austin
Text production by Jennifer Jepson Smith
Illustrations by © Marta Antelo/agoodson.com
Author photo by Cinthya Zuniga

Storey books are available at special discounts when purchased in bulk for premiums and sales promotions as well as for fund-raising or educational use. Special editions or book excerpts can also be created to specification. For details, please call 800-827-8673, or send an email to sales@storey.com.

Storey Publishing
210 MASS MoCA Way
North Adams, MA 01247
storey.com

Printed in China through World Print
10 9 8 7 6 5 4 3 2 1

Library of Congress Cataloging-in-Publication Data on file

What Is Mindfulness?

**Mindfulness is about noticing
what's happening — right here, right now.**
We can discover so much, just by paying attention!

Mindfulness helps us explore how we feel.
Different places and spaces can
make us feel certain ways. When we
go on mindful explorations, like
the ones in this book, we learn a lot about
ourselves and about the world
around us. So get ready, explorer.

Let's go!

Be a
Mindful Explorer!

Anyone can be a mindful explorer. All you need is **your attention** and **your breath**. With these two tools, you can go on all types of mindful adventures, even in the places you visit every day.

Breathe

Focus

How Will It Help?

The world can be confusing and scary. Sometimes it can feel like things are happening all around us and there's nothing we can do.

Mindfulness is a way to choose how to respond when something happens to us. We can pause, take a deep breath, and decide what we want to do next. It might not make the **anger**, **fear**, or **sadness** go away. But sometimes it can help us feel a bit better.

Fear

Calm

Anger

Let's Practice

Rise and Shine

It feels good to **stretch** right after getting out of bed. See how big you can shine through your chest, your arms, and your smile!

1 **Stand tall!**
Feet apart!

2 **Stretch your arms** up and out.

3 **Shine your fingers** by spreading them wide.

4 **Take a big breath** through your nose and into your chest.

5 **Breathe out** through your mouth.

Hello, Sunshine

The sun is up, and there's lots to do and see! Let's get our bodies moving as we **get ready** to start the day.

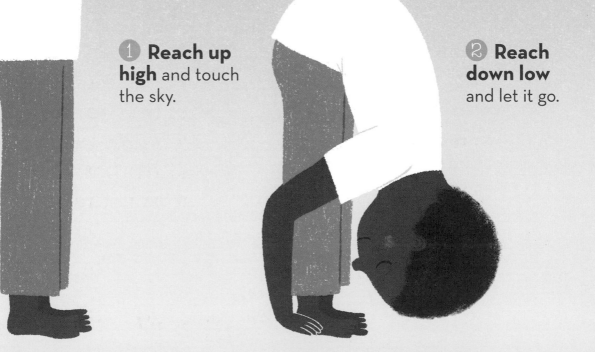

1 **Reach up high** and touch the sky.

2 **Reach down low** and let it go.

③ **Jump** like a frog into Downward Dog.

④ **Bring your belly low**, nice and slow.

⑤ **Lift your chest**, but not the rest.

⑥ Then **press back** to Downward Dog, and **relax . . .**

Do this exercise as many times as you want. Just remember to rest a little before you start again.

Check Your Inner Weather

What's the weather like in your **mind** and **body** today?

Is it **bright** and **sunny** in your heart?

Twisty like a tornado in your belly?

Foggy in your mind?

That's okay!

Remember, you are like the sky. You are **bigger** than any rain cloud or storm that is passing through you.

Once you **name your feelings**, you can choose how you want to respond.

Are We Here Yet?

Can't wait to get where you are going? Try to **notice what is happening** around you right now instead of worrying about where you will be.

Where are you?

Look around.

What **colors and shapes** are passing by?

Are you sitting **up high or underground** on a subway?

Is it **quiet or noisy**?

What do you **smell**?

Can you **touch both feet** to the floor?

Can you let your body **sink deeper** into your seat?

Is it a **smooth** ride?

Bumpy?

Snack Break

Next time you are about to have a snack
or a meal, **take a deep breath** and **find a seat**.
Get ready to go on an exploration . . .

Take a good look at your food.

What **colors** do you see?
How many **shapes** do you see?
How does the food **smell**?

Lettuce smells fresh and green.

Carrot sticks are orange rectangles.

Tomatoes are red circles.

Now, close your eyes and take a bite.

CRUNCH

What **sounds** do you make as you munch?

JUICY

What does it **feel** like in your mouth?

SALTY

What **tastes** are happening?

TRY THIS!
As you eat, ask yourself,
WHAT AM I GRATEFUL FOR?

Eat slowly, chewing and swallowing before taking another bite.

Take 5

Feeling jittery before trying something new? Take **deep breaths** to get calm. Then do your best.

1 **Breathe in** through your nose for five slow counts.

2 Then, slowly, **breathe out** through your mouth.

1 2 3 4 5   5 4 3 2 1

3 **Repeat** until you're ready!

TRY THIS!

Count on your fingers.
BREATHE while moving one finger at a time.

Take a big breath and fill your belly up like a balloon. Feel yourself float up to the sky!

Then let your breath out in a big sigh and settle back to the ground.

I Am Royalty

No matter where you are, or where you are from, you are destined for great things — like the king or queen of a kingdom! This is a practice to help you feel like the **strong leader** you are becoming.

Find a seat and close your eyes.

1 Imagine sitting **tall** on your throne, wearing an imaginary crown.

2 **Lift** your chin and chest.

3 Let your shoulders **relax** downward.

4 **Breathe in** through your nose.

5 **Think** about the people you admire — all the **kings and queens** that have come before you.

6 **Breathe out** through your mouth, remembering that you, too, are **royalty**.

Send Love

We see and talk to many people during the day.
Some are friends, and some are strangers.
Use these thoughts and words to send them all
love and **kindness**.

Start with yourself.

Take a **deep breath**.

Then, in a whisper or silently,
say the following words:

*May **I** be happy,*

*May **I** be well,*

*May **I** be
safe and sound.*

Now focus on
someone you know.

Send them the same
love and **kindness**
that you gave yourself:

May **you** be happy,

May **you** be well,

May **you** be
safe and sound.

Now, think of the
whole wide world
and everyone in it.

May **we all** be happy,

May **we all** be well,

May **we all** be
safe and sound.

Cats and Cows

When we sit too long, we often slouch. Here's a **movement** you can do right in your chair to **stretch** out your back.

First be a cow.

Sit up tall, and **puff out** your chest.

Lift your chin up high.

Breathe into your belly.

Then curl your back like a cat.

Pull your shoulders toward your ears.

Bring your chin to your chest.

Breathe out with a *hisssssss*.

Do your cats and cows
a few times, until
you feel nice and loose!

Explore Nature

Outside there's so much to **feel**, **smell**, **hear**, and **see**. Try to notice everything about nature that you can! It doesn't matter if you are in the city or in the woods — nature is everywhere.

Can you **feel** the earth under your feet?

Can you **feel** the air around you?

Do you **feel** the sun smiling on your skin?

Can you **feel** rain?

Do you **see** any trees or flowers?

What do you **smell**?

What do you **hear**?

TRY THIS!
When you're inside, see if you can remember all your FAVORITE THINGS about being outside in nature.

Move like an Owl

Have you been looking at a screen for a while? Time to take a break! Try these owl **movements** to to keep your **eyes** healthy and your **neck** and **shoulders** loose.

Owls can't move their eyes, so they have to move their necks in order to see all around themselves . . .

Move your head to look up. Look down. **Look all around.**

Bring your shoulders **up** to your ears, and then let them **drop**.

Shut your eyes, then open them wide.

Stretch out your wings!

Take a **big breath** and fill up your chest.

Let it out and close your eyes.

Take a Mind Picture

Each day, you see so many cool things. Take a picture with your mind so you can **remember** what you see.

Choose something that catches your eye.

Look closely.

What does your picture **sound** like?

What **colors** do you **see**?

What is **moving**?

What is **still**?

What does your picture **smell** like?

Breathe in.
Pull this picture into your body.

Breathe out to take the picture.

**Now,
close your eyes.**
Can you still see
the picture you
just took?

TRY THIS!

When you lie down and close your eyes at night,
try looking at the MIND PICTURES you took today.

Grow like a Tree

We have so much to learn from the trees! They are **tall** and **strong** and **peaceful**. Let's practice being a beautiful tree.

1. **Stand tall** and strong on both feet, like a tree trunk.

2. **Press** one foot into the ground and imagine growing roots.

3. **Place** your other foot on your leg below your knee.

4. **Feel** yourself **grow** from the top of your head.

5. **Bring** your hands together in front of your heart.

6. **If you want to grow even taller,** bring your arms up to the sky like branches.

TRY THIS!
Can you BEND and SWAY in the breeze?

Close your eyes and count how many different sounds you can hear.

Legs Up, Cool Down

Getting mad can heat you up! The Legs Up pose can help you **cool down**.

How could they do that?

ARGH!

I'M MAD

I'm so upset!

I'M ANGRY

GAH!

I'M MAD

GRR!

It's not fair!

I'M ANGRY

They were so mean to me!

I'M MAD

ARGH!

1. **Sit** on the floor facing a wall.

2. **Lie down** on the floor, and place the bottoms of your feet on the wall.

3. **Walk** your feet up the wall until your toes are above your head.

4. **Place** one hand on your **belly**.

5. **Place** the other hand on your **heart**.

6. **Take** big breaths in and out until your body feels **cooler** and more **relaxed**.

Breathe like a Walrus

When we get angry, our bodies can get tight.
Pretend you are a **slow**, **calm** walrus to relax
your body and your mind, too.

1 **Let** the sides of your face get **heavy**.

2 **Imagine** your front teeth growing into long walrus tusks.

3 **Stretch** your hands open like flippers, and **swim** through the sea.

HARRUMPH!

Take a big breath in through your nose, and **harrumph!** out of your walrus mouth.

Help

Care

Draw your knees into your chest and give yourself a big hug. Say thank you to YOU for all that you do.

Play

Study

Clean

Proud like a Lion

Imagine you are a big, brave lion in the grasslands. You are **proud** of who you are and who you will be.

 Sit tall.

2 Feel your **lion's mane** grow up to the sky.

3 Place your big lion **paws** on each knee.

4 Take a **big breath** in through your nose.

5 **Open** your mouth **wide** and stick out your tongue.

6 **Breathe out like a lion!**

ROARRRR!

Pose like a Superhero

We are all superheroes, even when we aren't wearing a cape. Let's pretend to be superheroes to feel **big** and **brave**.

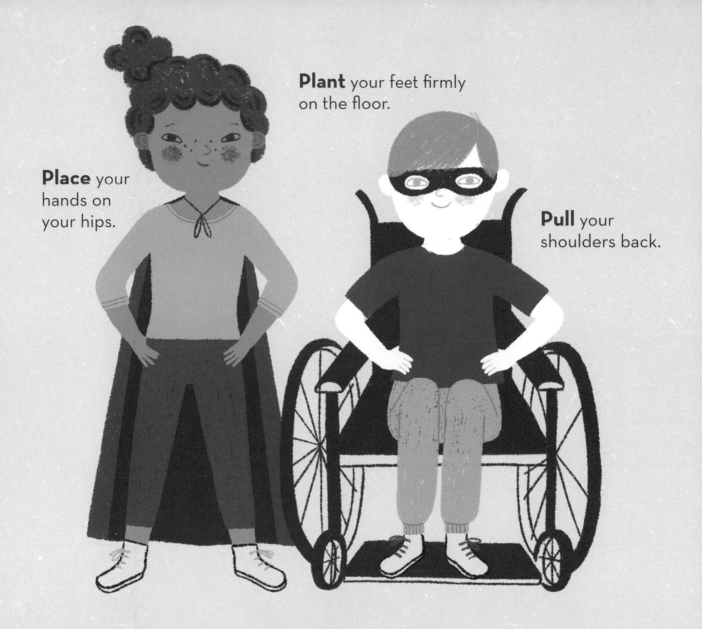

Plant your feet firmly on the floor.

Place your hands on your hips.

Pull your shoulders back.

Be tall like the hero you are, ready to save the day!

TRY THIS!

Think of something you are really good at.
WHAT IS YOUR INNER SUPERPOWER?

Flower and Candle Breath

It's okay to feel **worried** or **anxious**. But anxiety can be scary, like a very mean dog or loud thunder. Sometimes, flower and candle breathing can help you calm down.

1 **Pretend** you are holding a flower in one hand.

What **color** is it?

What does it **smell** like?

2 **Pretend** you are holding a candle in your other hand.

What **color** is it?

How **tall** is it?

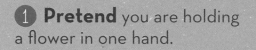

3 **Smell** the flower with a big sniff in through your nose.

4 **Blow out** the candle with a long, soft breath from your mouth.

Keep practicing until you feel calm.

Move like a Jellyfish

Jellyfish go with the flow. Their soft bodies help them stay calm, even when they feel scared or worried.

Can you **let go** and **flow** like a jellyfish?

1. **Stand** with your knees bent.

2. **Fold** forward over your legs so your chest reaches toward your knees.

3. **Make** your arms and legs **loose** like a jellyfish.

4. **Sway** from side to side.

5. **Breathe in** and out as you move.

Do Nothing Pose

Take a break! It's good for your body and your mind, especially if you are having a tough day.

1 **Lie down** on the ground, a bed, or a couch.

2 **Relax** each part of your body, from your toes to the top of your head.

3 **Relax** your **feet**. Relax your **legs**. Relax your **arms**. Relax your **neck**. Relax your **mouth** . . . and your **eyes** . . . and even your **nose**.

Let your thoughts pass by like clouds in the sky.

Don't try to stop them, and **don't hold on** to them.

Do nothing.

Place one hand on your heart and count every heartbeat.

THUMP THUMP

123

How fast is it beating?

Slow like a snail?

...or a **turtle**?

Quick like a **bunny**?

Speedy like a **cheetah**?

Zippy like a car?

Bedtime Blastoff

Sometimes, even though you've turned out the lights and climbed into bed, your mind is still full.

Let's make room for **sleep**.

1 **Imagine** a big, shiny rocket ship.

2 **Fill it up** with your thoughts.

3 **Close** the door, and **blast off**!

4 **Watch** the rocket shoot toward the stars and go farther and farther away.

5 **Picture it getting smaller** in the big black sky.

And smaller

and smaller . . .

6 Finally, all that's left is a clear sky, filled with shining stars . . . a whole universe of space for sleepy **dreams**.

Sleepy Snuggles

Choose a stuffed animal, a blanket, or another favorite object to be your friend.

Help your friend get ready for sleep.

Lie on your back.

Place your friend gently on your belly.

Take a big breath into your belly, and watch your friend **rise to the sky**.

Let that big breath out through your mouth, and watch your friend **settle into sleep**.

Keep breathing slowly. Fill your belly like a balloon. Watch your friend move up and down until you're both **calm** and **settled** for bedtime.

All Quiet Inside

As you lie in bed, notice the sounds around you. Where are they coming from?

Now, let's notice the sounds **inside you**.

Close your eyes and **tune in** to different parts of your body.

Can you hear your feet getting tired?

Can you hear your legs relax?

Listen to your body get ready to fall asleep.

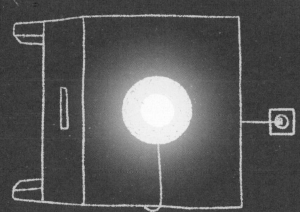